OWELE

ALSO BY SIHLE NTULI

CHAPBOOKS
Rumblin' (uHlanga, 2020)
The Nation (River Glass Books, 2023)

COLLECTIONS
Stranger (Aerial Publishing, 2015)
Zabalaza Republic (Botsotso, 2023)

OWELE

IZINKONDLO
POEMS

SIHLE NTULI

UHLANGA
2025

Owele
© Sihle Ntuli, 2025, all rights reserved

First published in Durban, South Africa by uHlanga in 2025
UHLANGAPRESS.CO.ZA

Distributed outside South Africa by the African Books Collective
AFRICANBOOKSCOLLECTIVE.COM

ISBN: 978-1-0370-5172-2

Cover and inside photographs by Samora Chapman
Cover design by Nick Mulgrew

Edited by Nick Mulgrew, Sandile Ngidi and Musawenkosi Cabe
Typesetting by Nick Mulgrew
Proofread by Musawenkosi Cabe and Jennifer Jacobs

The body text of this book is set in Garamond Premier Pro and Hacky

ACKNOWLEDGEMENTS

I would like to acknowledge the Centre for Stories, Western Australia for their support during the production of this manuscript through the Patricia Kailis Fellowship.

Earlier versions of the poems that appear in this collection have appeared previously in *ADDA stories*, *Ake Review*, *Apogee Journal*, *Bennington Review*, *Evergreen Review*, *Poetry Wales*, *Tint Journal*, *Ubwali Literary Magazine*, *Wasafiri*, and on the website of the University of Georgia.

⓪

Ngithanda ukuqala ngokubonga uNkulunkulu, uThixo ngempela ukhona. I would like to dedicate this book to the city of Durban, UNESCO's first City of Literature in Africa.

With all humility, I'd like to express my deep and sincere gratitude to Nick Mulgrew for believing in this vision and seeing it through. Congratulations on over 10 years of uHlanga – from featuring in the very first book in 2014 to now has been an absolute honour and a privilege; thank you for helping me feel at home and navigating through what can often be a difficult South African literary scene.

Thank you to George Kailis, Caroline and Robert Wood, and the Centre for Stories, with special mention to Ange, Calvin, Caitlin, Danielle, John (Mateer), Pranay, Sara and especially Vuma – thank you for taking very good care of me during my time in Perth, I am so grateful.

To my fellow writers: thank you Maneo Mohale, T. J. Benson, Henneh Kyereh Kwaku, Jeremy Karn and Manti Moila for having both direct and indirect involvement in some of these poems; each of your artistic journeys continue to inspire me.

Ngibonga kakhulu to iwele lami uSipho who inspired the collection. Thank you to other key people in my life who helped me a lot, including Mlangost, Hlase, Andile, Monde (Mrs Porter!), Pepper, the Simango Brothers (Ron & Sam), Mncedisi, Mind, O'Ryan, Themba Mwelase and Lumumba.

Rest in peace to Pinkie Tekane (umamkhulu), Edna Ntuli (ugogo) Lucky Malope, Karabo Makwela (Morpheus) – your memories live on within me always.

I'd like to say thank you to the isiZulu editors of this collection, firstly to Sandile Ngidi – it was quite an ambitious ask, though your patience and understanding has ultimately seen us through. To Musawenkosi Cabe, thank you for the unwavering support, even through a very important transition in your life; the contribution you've made here is invaluable.

A huge thank you to Aslam Mayat, whose continued presence and support has been key to any good thing I do in this world. And last, a special thanks to the big homie Abongile Silonga – I appreciate the stability you continue to provide for me.

— S. N.

CONTENTS

UMNGENI *11*

Qala *12*

Scapegoat *14*

Thuli *15*

Ars Poetica as Bildungsroman *16*

Nganekwane *17*

Mother *18*

NCOME *21*

Langa *22*

Reparations *23*

Darkie Fiction *25*

In The Blood *26*

The Infinite Pursuit of Booty *27*

Symposia at Bernard's Quartyard *28*

OHLANGA *31*

Tshala *32*

Ars Poetica In Deep Contemplation *33*

Shade *34*

December *35*

Belly *36*

Our Neighbourhood Tends to Its Grief Through an Everlasting Feast of Libations *37*

MSUNDUZI *39*

Linga *40*

Ars Poetica of the Blue Note *41*

Magezangobisi *43*

The Etymology of Thanda/Thando   44
Bekungasafudumele   47
Parables of Bone & Cotton   48
THUKELA   51
Lamba   52
Mfecane   53
Kasala (for a first-born twin)   54
Lenge   55
Owele   56
Isibongo   57
UMBILO   59
Xolani   60
Ars Poetica as a Musical Interpolation of the Thunder   61
Azanian Abecedarian (with Eyes)   63
Baw Baw (One for the Black Sheep)   64
In The Presence of Ocean Water   65
Swimming versus Drowning   66
ULWANDLE LWASENDIYA   69
Lunga   70
You Are the Elders Now   71
Aubade to the Natural Light & The Revelation of Love   72
Mamkhulu   73
Ode to the Wind Blowing Gently Over Our Wounds   74
The Brother Moves On   75
Ngizizwa Ngingenwa Uvalo   78

NOTES   80

Kubo labo abasibonayo isidingo
sokubhekana ngqo! nesimnyama sabo

UMNGENI

sondelani sizwe saba nsundu,

   lomfula usuka kude
   kudala uhamba,
   usuyafika

abadala baziletha izexwayiso,
kudala besho bethi
   zingane zakwethu qaphelani:
   ningalinge nivume
   imiphimbo yenu
   yome nithule,
   ikakhulukazi
   manibona
   umnyakazo emanzini
   ningalinge nilinde,
   nivele nishone khona
   kungabi namazwi
   asalela emphinjeni.

mfula osondela ngasolwandle
siyakuncenga, sicela usicacisele,
sifuna ukuzwa ngawe:
sibuza kuwe, sithi wena uthule uthini?
amaPutukezi edlula, egudla ngakuwena,

   mlomo kaDaGama waphuza kuwe Mngeni
   izisebenzi zakhe seziqondane ngqo nokoma,
   umusa wakho Mngeni wabasindisa,
   isizwe saba nsundu sona sasala nokoma.

Qala

soft origin of bone, of
breath breathed into
bone, the holding of
the book / the bone
a foreshadowing

in the moments
our ancestors provide warning,
everything will rest
on the positioning
of bones

of terror
ubizo colliding with the baritone
that rose the Genesis,
hands come down harder
on dark skin / cowhide

mercy ease our pain
khala sghubu
ngegama likabani?
our eyes looked
everywhere for you

through black church / mgido
drummed
    (into us)
how our chests feel
beaten
by our fear

Scapegoat

One of us will have to lead the ritual.
The other will grab the horns & drag the goat inside
while its hooves slide begrudgingly across the ceramic floor.

From here the goat will be moved to a room.
In this room it will be presented to the ancestors as an offering
while an elder puts a match to impepho & waits for it to burn.

One of us will have to speak on behalf of the family.
Both of us will need to keep the smoke from entering our lungs
& should the goat sneeze from the fumes none of us can laugh.

There is a certain gravitas in the moments while speaking
to our divine forebears, watching over us, from under us.
One elder even agonises about our rituals under threat.

From the corner of both our eyes
to the corner of our grandfather's courtyard,
we witness the goat being positioned into a spot for the ritual.

We will both hesitate when the head of the house is asked to step forward.
The elders who say whiteness has become us will feel vindicated.
The one who steps up will have a point to prove.

Both of us will learn about separation
when an elder points at a bone on the neck of the goat
& tells the head to liberate the body.

Thuli

umlando wakithi waqala ngothuli,
uze uzibuze kambe yini le
eyenza imilenze yabo
ibambe ijubane?
amehlo abomvu
songo lokufa
khala nhliziyo
jika zinyoni
uyafisa, ukwesaba
kusindisa umzimba,
amehlo alibonile ilanga
lishona, asebonile ukuthi
kulento ababhekana nayo
bekungenzeka bengasindi

Ars Poetica as Bildungsroman

& if a poem   should form   under a dark cloud
& shadows   beneath   a burdensome silence
in lieu of floodgates   a drought   of newborn eyes
in absence   of a first cry   piercing through
a living room   full   of breathing
a disruptor   of silence   a sharp pitched tone
cutting   through tabula rasa   & from this opening
will emerge the virgin voice   *what would it mean*
to not know   *where this voice*   *was coming from?*

a seed planted in the soul   a poem with a promise
to bloom   *in whose hands*   *rests the potential*
to bloom?   the speaker   or divinity
their abundant names   yet still unable to distinguish
who is most worthy   to be deemed   *Creator*?

nature versus nurture   free will versus determinism
    how soft the soil of devotion
       how hard the clay of disdain
what of bones forming the opening line?
will it break?   *will it be strong enough to hold?*

when rain falls   touches ground   the sound it makes
    a semblance of structure
to the bones hardening   to the firming of a voice
the tone of my speaker   in search of words   buried
under years of denial   a root making itself known
as one amongst us   a poem reaching for
the pulse of it   *how much more*   *breathing*
will it take   *until we find meaning?*

Nganekwane

amabhodlela aluhlaza aimed
down throats, gcwala mkhaba
fill with gwebu, round the outer edges,
reaffirm the bulge, bhodlani milomo,
khalani makhala, power stench

beer-breathed middle-aged men
blow down umshayamoya,
lowdown caucus, raucous madoda
bought offense to his head
pensive man

the one donning orange,
lime green reflector vest,
crouching tiger hidden ~~dragon~~
storyteller pose, inganekwane
chose him, compelled him
to share his story,
the one he held so firm
so close to his chest

bamphendula bathi
we-le-le! inganekwane uyasibhedela
yasho indakazo, poured down,
viral clip emptied, the tragedy
of our storytellers laughed out,
they didn't even let him finish
he ended right where he began
just as he was telling them
that *a man and his daughter were
walking in the forest...*

Mother

your tongue
inside my mouth
held down

I barely hear you
as I speak
inside // thick coats

of theirs, the taste
like cotton
uniformed
my ironed tongue
uncreased by
echoing clicks

I wonder
if I still have enough
of you saved

for the day
I walk barefoot
in the rural rustic land
of Zulu

how else might
I let relatives
long lost

know in words
that I've become
more accustomed

to shoes, that the
bareness of grass
fields hurt my feet?

NCOME

ngezikhathi zakudala, amabhunu esaqala
ukulwa nabansundu, kubangwa umhlaba

kuyo lempi bayiqamba ngokuthi:
    'Impi yomfula wegazi'
okwakuliwa maqondana nomfula
lona abadala uma bewubiza
bethi,   *'Ncome!'*
ubusabela

      igazi latheleka
      umfula washintsha,
      umbala waba bomvu
      lavaleka igama lomfula
      wemuka nayo
      imphefumulo yamabutho

silonda valeka / emva kwayo yonke leminyaka
lutho ukuphola / mfula wase Ncome
kuzoze kube nini / bekubiza ngalo okungesilona

ukuqanjwa kwakho ngegazi lethu
kuyasithunuka namanje

Langa

uOusmane wakaSembène wabuza
wathi: kungani ngibe umajikanelanga,
ngihlale ngokubheka ilanga
mina ngokwami, ngiyilo ilanga!

Reparations
or, Our Word for 'Soil', 'Land', 'Earth' & 'World' Is One & The Same

SOIL

umkhulu was buried without his home returned to him

ropes carefully slid his casket down,
dressed in a woollen brown suit
arms crossed over his chest
coming together
from where all the hurt emanated

& sometimes
when I close my eyes
I can hear him

LAND

screaming, *where is the land?*
pleading for reparations owed by
oz'ndlebe z'khanya ilanga

often I have this dream
of umkhulu blowing on his saxophone

& for a moment I am unable to feel him
until I am drowning in a river flowing
from his eyes

EARTH

    & in an opening I find her spirit
    umamkhulu speaks to me
    about the sharpness of the earth
    'lomhlaba uyahlaba'
    or *this world is sharp*
    if only I had listened

    perhaps my skin would be as tough
    as her resolve
    how long will I be weary
    of the ones who sharpen our earth?
                in our culture
    when you say 'umhlaba'
    you are speaking of

WORLD

the piercing edge through our palms
& all that was taken from us

black hand civilising tar / wooden floors creaking underfoot
sounds of the unnatural / umkhulu long dead / unable to rest

because the isiZulu word for soil, land, earth are one & the same
the depths of a hole are as deep as the loss of our ancestors

our paths converge down below / & for us, AmaZulu,
the whole ordeal has been like losing our—

Darkie Fiction

choking,
        or a forearm raised, shielding a mouth amid the flames

              and ngamla should have known
change would come / blowing with the wind
must have thought it fiction / in disbelief / wondering
how a continent so dark / could have made the discovery
on their own / our illuminated homes
        in the wilderness / oral traditions of our myths
              as told by our foremothers
    before ondleb'zikhany' ilanga...
                before *they* came.

    oh, silenced songs of okhokho
who is to blame for your fading? / iz'thakezlo zethu turned
whispers / the weight of wilted flowers
    of leaves left fallen
              /
            in vast fields of wanting.

              lungs breathe in heat
        humidity / inside the neck / a dry spot
spreads
    thirst / unmerciful sun / a veld fire
        running down the bridge
      moving towards the chorus
        a smoke that reddened the chest
      that made the lungs feel like

                    burning.

In The Blood

is the river an honest mirror of our nature?
are still waters a reflection of us?

how deeply have we looked within us?
how has this happened to a body of water?

who took away the clear colour of the water?
who has left blood behind here?

why the denial of what was left here?
why so adamant that our hands are clean?

will a river let us know whose hands it has washed clean?
will truth reveal itself at the mouth of a river?

do harsh truths lie on the bed of this river?
is the river an honest mirror of our nature?

The Infinite Pursuit of Booty

& was it a hunger that compelled the move?
Nguni residue on mother tongue, could her lips feel his
    even through the lies? how far were his legs prepared to walk / away
from the umbilical cords buried / beneath the plateaus of Mambilla?

home of the ones who stayed

    & if the story often told is one of a long journey
could their migration have been the first betrayal?
    not much has been said of a final gathering of the tribe
before their parting of ways / amid a glowing backdrop / the flame

        burning through / as fire took the place of a fallen sun

    while brass baritones battled to defeat a challenge made
a mysterious outcome / one we may never truly know / was it the victors
    or the losers who chose to walk? / were our foremothers silent
while remaining faithful to the feet forging a path to their new home?

    the search for sustenance continued / through footprints
left along the Atlantic coast / following rivers running south
    how could obaba bethu have known the potential of soil
if not for seeds from their loins scattered everywhere

    all that trust given to them to hold / as they blocked the sun
and could her intuition have foreshadowed / the downfall of man's integrity
    the unsatiable / a lust never-ending / a borderless pursuit of booty
the origin story of generations / of seeds planted deep inside the earth

        left to grow wildly from the roots

Symposia at Bernard's Quartyard

brother, if only you knew how this house came to be
& don't you ask me how I define *home* – at least not for now,
because your question is capable of moving me to tears.

& as we sit here on these empty Black Label crates,
consider how some have found *home* in cold barley,
coating throats in white foam, pacified pariahs of struggle

imagine if their Anglo-Saxon names were also forced upon us
just so others could feel at *home* – like umkhulu, denied
his birth name Shongani, becoming Bernard to the ones

who so forcefully removed him. brother, what I mean to say
is that KwaMashu was never our *home*, it was merely a place,
where his body landed after being thrown

his throne only claimed in the ceremony of his ancestral planting,
deep into the soil while his spirit was being returned *home*,
leaving the women of the house with the burden.

ugogo and her daughters worked hard to turn this house into a *home*,
this very house we've inherited – left to us after all but one died –
in their memory, may we ensure its integrity is preserved.

consider this house as compensation for the *home*
umkhulu lost – his clenching mind unable to let go before his soul did
with the kind of hurt that returns as soon as it is remembered.

what is *home* if our neighbours only speak to me in English,
oblivious to what the language has done?
& so your question about home is one that is hard to answer,

because when the pain comes, I always have to convince myself
that I am a man who cannot feel a thing – who will not feel
a thing – until suddenly I am overcome by the urge to disappear.

OHLANGA

ngesintu,
uma sikhuluma ngohlanga
siqonde ukuthi leyo ndawo
sonke esaphuma khona,
kwi lempi yezinhlanga
siyakhumbula
kuliwa maduze
nodonga lwakho,
nathi singazi
sibheke ngakuphi,
samangala usushintsha
imibala, kuyithina esakwenza
okubi, ngokungcola
esakulethela

Tshala

sibonga zona
izandla ezasithambela,
zinolwazi ukuthi ukuvuthwa
nobudala akusiyona into eyodwa,

sibonga bona
ababa nolwazi, ukuthi izimbali
ziphathwa kanjani, ngoba
iningi lethu siyizimbewu
ezaphazamiseka

Ars Poetica In Deep Contemplation

palms not stable enough
to hold running water

bones of the fingers
eventually feel pain
holding on too long

the interrogation of the soul begins
with the eyes of a page
staring blankly back towards a face

the purpose of mirrors is not only to reflect
the face, but perhaps to look
even deeper, beneath the illusion

the sounds of trouble are not only heard by the ears

                in deep contemplation
excavating   dormant   awakening

mouth : a pink inner lining
mouth : a sharp thing hidden inside
mouth : a gentle song to calm the blood

                & is it all because
        my silences are no longer golden?

                in deep contemplation
burial   resurrection   eternity

Shade
or, The Revelation of All Our Neighbourhood Has Lost

in our neighbourhood the roosters have chosen silence, refusing to receive the glorious rise of the sun with us. the generation who formed a bond with trees remain haunted by tree stumps, my grandmother among them. often I have heard it said that the living keep the spirit of the dead with them, holding it inside, here, there & everywhere. in our neighbourhood, only the sound systems refuse to die. the presence of an elder no longer lulls subwoofers to sleep; *& this is how we lose them*, some of us will say. our word for shade & dignity is one & the same. the gathered wood we burn another of our losses. *& is this how we surrendered them*? our minds were too stubborn to yield, as if the harsh rays of the sun would never hurt us again. so forgetful that even the trees serve a purpose.

December

as if the sunshine could not burn hot enough.
the flame, the name summer itself
so unassuming. today I woke with rays,
sharp edges pointed, towards me

threatening harm. I dream of ice
cold on the tongue, silencing the thirst,
smothering the conundrums of half-full-
half-empty, a glass I once shattered

only my mouth left open,
gathering rain, neck
as a waterfall. the mirages
of December have come.

there is no more water here,
only beer now. all the years
I turn down temptation
soften my resolve.

I wonder
who I would become
if I was reckless enough
to risk it all, to throw it all away?

Belly

/ˈbeli/
noun

1. uGwede's body shamed, by a protester, who complained about the protrusion of his gut, questioning its audacity to hang, hollering, echoing: *have you seen it!*

2. an entourage moves through a nightclub in their neon blue skin, once brown, altered by vivid strobe lights; eyeballs left a luminous white & blinking

3. a camera makes sure to not go below the abdomen of the soul singer, during the idol worship of an Adonis and the *Untitled* video that drove him insane

4. resting below my ribs, ballad of the midriff played softly to the soul, to my soul back to life, a deep study in reflection, staring at a mirror

Our Neighbourhood Tends to Its Grief Through an Everlasting Feast of Libations

Mashu / your grief so heavy / the lord of motion stops moving the wheels / of an SAB truck / dead as if to force it to observe your pain & please / don't you make the mistake of deeming this a failure of an engine / instead let it be known / abaphansi deemed it fit / for the breakdown of this delivery truck / for it was fate that decided this would happen right here / to match a freshness of red wounds in textures of our gathered sorrow / heavy is the ~~head~~ vessel / leaving behind thickened scars on tar / anointing black lines on roads curved as the cursive divine sign left behind / holy as a halting suddenly / in the middle of the openness / all the more vulnerable as the crowd trickles in

& gathers / on the scent of blood / tongues coil seductively around the wound & lick / in search of comfort / consoling slow hum of the engine / a harmonised montage: deep in the heart of summer crate-sized burdens released / onto the shoulders of amaphikini naboTakalani who held tough / amajita nabo mama / taking the load off wheels of the unmoving / all desires fed / soul of the engine freed drifting to a soft death

Our neighbourhood tends to its grief through an everlasting feast of libations / for abadala are all dead now / the households are run by crooked children / the spines reluctant to align / unwilling to uphold lineage / heavy gravitas of last names / the only thing our throats tend to do is swallow / Mashu is the great flooding our comrades in too deep / so all we ever see is drowning

MSUNDUZI

hamba moya yezithandwa zami
yona ehleli nami, ayingidedeli

lude uhambo lobugwala bami
mfula hamba, konke sekuyaphela

ngifa phansi kwaleli phupho lami
amazwi ami esefela emlanjeni

lapho kungathi ngiwela phansi
ngesifuba ngiphinde ngishayeke

ngiyesaba ngaphakathi
Mgungundlovu, ngeke ngisasondela

Linga

ngabona sengivinjwe ngomama,
isiphongo sami sigcwele ezabo izandla,

bethi, *nkosi* mkhiphe wonke lamadimoni
mbusise *baba!* lomkhuleko uyawudinga

sizwe ngemibuzo yakhe ehlaza
eqonde kuwe *nkosi*, sabona ukuthi
ngempela, usathane uyamlinga

Ars Poetica of the Blue Note

   how long before the blues come for me again?

the poem as an instrument lulling
humming sound of the soul unquieted
unused notes tucked inside
the throat, dangling chandelier
of unsaids, a lingering soundlessness
my sacrifice, my suffocation
the note still forming

   how long before the jazz of uncertainty sets in?

in the intimacy of mouths
& aerophone, the coming
together of wind blowing gently
from lungs, a delicateness
seeking out the poem
from inside, waiting behind eyes,
cocooning hypnotism,
hiding, two black dots

how long until I emerge from the cave of the soul?

slow-motioned fingers feel out
for realism, surrealism,
human metronome, temporal lobes
the only concern is stimulation
only for so long could I appeal to the woke
soon even they will tire

& there I will be all on my own,
the magic diluted by restlessness,
left desperately searching for the poem

Magezangobisi

ngizwe umoya wami ukukhalela,
  engathi ngingakusondeza
ngikuhlebele, ngithi *'dudlu!'*

The Etymology of Thanda/Thando
after E'mon Lauren

[thanda/thando]

a Nguni word meaning *love*
though its meaning tends to get confused with *like*
because there can be no clear way to tell

as in: this kind of *love* is so abundant it will not be beholden
         to thresholds   of how much   or how little

[thanda] – used to describe a subject / object of love

for this variation to be properly pronounced / one must begin with
a common exclamation / used by magicians

thanda is pronounced similar to
tada! / but instead of the enchanting *da!*
use a more subdued *duh*
(as in: we already know the magician's tricks)
we include an 'n' and between the magic
tada becomes *thanda*

as in: ngiyabathanda abantu bami abangamaNguni
or *I love my Nguni people*

& so let us pretend this 'n'
between *tha* & *da* stands
for *nguni:*

subject of my love
object of my love / my people
so forgetful of our migration
from the west of the sub-Sahara
amid black civil war so divisive

& so again / let us pretend the 'n' / between the magic
stands for *nguni* / as we wonder about the hunger that holds us back

      [thando] – used to describe a type / kind / nature of love

for this variation / we remain in our founding exclamation of magic
the '*do*' in thando pronounced as '*doe*'
as in *dough*
as in money

in this case / a qualitative comprehension of the *love*

as in: uthando lamaNguni seliqalile ukuphela
or *the love between Nguni peoples is beginning to fade*

& here / the 'n'
will no longer stand
for *nguni*

because they have closed the door
on the *type / kind / nature*
of love:

seeds of division sown / each side so willing / to set fire to the crops of another / not realising our common hunger as we approach our shared destiny of ashes

Bekungasafudumele

ngisale nesikhumba sezingalo zami
ngiqhaqhazela, ngifa amakhaza

Parables of Bone & Cotton

in the parable of the forgotten backbone

formless in retrospect
a family that calls you sensitive
the quiet child you always were
a mouth that held the word / *love* / for so long
the tongue lost the strength to say it
not even to his own mother
how does your body live with all that guilt?
fingers pull in search of piety
a thread of cotton unravelling

in the parable of a stitched thread of cotton

of all that could come undone
concealed beneath a tongue / fertile soil of mother
born with your mouth closed / your purpose in life is to open
& grow amid the never-ending threat
the need to decisively deal with that shadow
a single cotton thread / hovering / index finger
& thumb / come together & pull / painful
how you make yourself small / painless
how they blinked themselves blind

in the parable of wind blowing over bone

falling over yourself
for all your life you've watched rivers
your will so easily questioned by a breeze
you forget to ask / this teaching river for its name
oh, how time softens bone / & a breeze that tucked its way
inside your heart / blew itself away / only to return
as a gale / one you still know
and you fear / this time
it has returned / to finish you

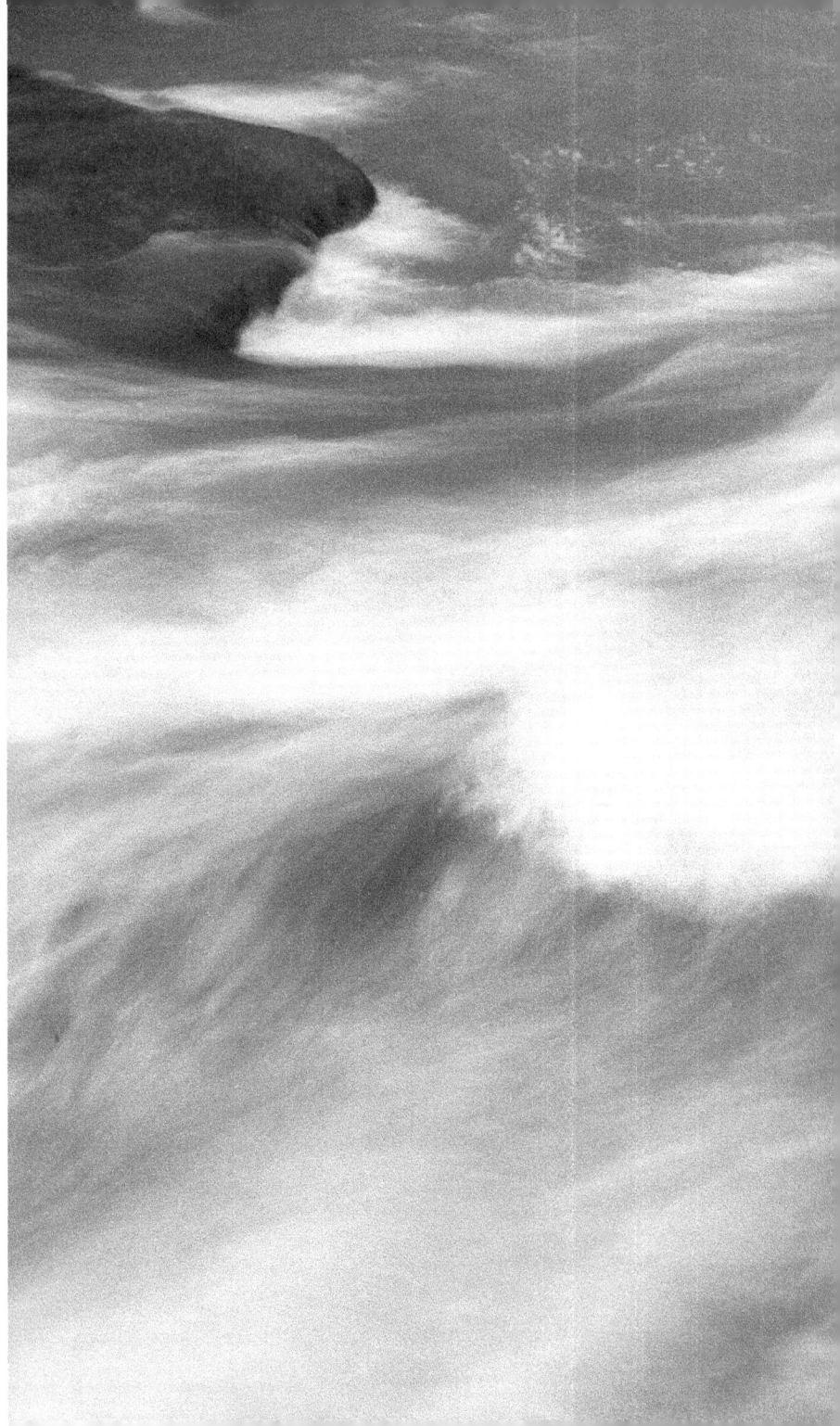

THUKELA

bafo, kambe abakithi bazizwa benjani,
bebalekela amazim'zimu,
kuwo lomlando wethu
bayasho bathi: sabonakala
ngefu lezintuli, lapho saqanjwa
ngokwenzakala kubalekwa.
isiqalo sethu lesi.

wele lami, ngike ngiphuphe
konke okubi okwenzeke kimi
lokhu okwangisondeza nokufa
lokhu okwadala abakithi bebaleke
ngike ngizibuze   yini eyadala ukwesaba?
kambe ilona lodwa   ifa abasishiyela lona

Lamba

usubuka elakho iwele,
ulibona linakho konke
lokho nawe okulambele.

Mfecane
after Maneo Mohale

the first act begins
while competing for the love of a single mother

on the subject of twins
African myth has always been divided

how come hands pick flowers
to sever from soil   sacrifice is the gift

and the curse is loving your brother
hoping for the return of a version you remember

                amid the unbearable heat of a moment
                      the second act begins

          with the words I form against you and thrust
                that turn against me and conquer

                    & when I ask you about water
                    the thickness of our blood

                    your spear is the rebuttal
                  that never leaves your throat

Kasala (for a first-born twin)

mfana ka Thandiwe, heir of Themba,
your river of life so full
all hope flows towards you
pointing to the sun
& yet for some reason
you are still so reluctant to take
your final form as an ocean

descendant of Godide, Mphemba,
Ndlela ka Sompisi,
your will so intentional
foot stepping forming pathways
tall grass swaying from your wind
    & even a second-born twin
is so inclined to blindly follow you
into the dark confines of your cave

sibonga oMwelase ka Ndlovu,
soles of your two feet
in rich dialogue with soil
on long walks to find yourself
we acknowledge the blood flowing within you
like a compromise of two rivers merged
bless Ntuli and Mwelase clans running
inside of you, forging an heir so worthy
of admiration and love,
graciously received
in abundance.

Lenge

after our kin evaded
the relentless hunger of amazim'zimu
abadla abantu / the cannibals
unable to devour their flesh

abakwa Ntuli ran towards
the mountainous terrain
of Lenge, & there they would stay
for a period, inside dark caves

hidden amid night terrors
the rumble of hunger pangs

& so, brother, the question
is one of lines,
because how could we know
what it means to truly starve

Owele

Ngesilungu: uma kuzalwa amawele
                     yena lo ophuma kuqala
                     kuthiwa uyena omdala

Ngesintu: uma kuzalwa amawele
                     yena lo ophume okokugcina
                     sithi uyena omdala

                     wele lami, le, angeke sayixazulula ngokuphelele!
                     umuntu nomuntu, ngezenzo zakhe
                     izona ezizoveza

Isibongo

umlando wasendlini outlines the origins of our family name
brother, I struggle to move past this one part that haunts me

my mind unable to get over the one part bothering me
the mystery of what our ancestors were running from

upon further tracing of what they were running from
through broad depths of Zulu so capable of hiding things

isithakazelo ~~of what is told between blood lines~~ conceals things
the myth of what took place inside the dark caves of Lenge

is there any truth to what they said happened at Lenge?
were our ancestors the ones running from the cannibals?

were our ancestors the ones who became the cannibals?
I have nightmares of the sides of their mouths lined with blood

my mouth left open, questioning the origins of my blood, while
umlando wasendlini outlines the origins of our family name

UMBILO

ngobani abalethe
imfucuza egcwele
umfula, zonke
izinhlanga ziyakhombana,
lapho seziyaduma
zivutha, amazwi
ephoselwa phezulu,
kungasekho ngisho
noyedwa osele
phansi, ezozwa
lomfula, igama
lawo ulivuma

Xolani

mazehle izikhali, nehlise nomoya
omunye nomunye aphiwe indlebe

Ars Poetica as a Musical Interpolation of the Thunder

    holding   breathing   waiting
    pleading   for deliverance from
    a dark cloud hanging

      count from the lightning
                to the undistinguishable
                          crash
              clashing clouds
            approaching
        percussion
    in my skull
      tension
          declension
                running

    the form of this poem shaped
    by the inner child
      that could never face
                ~~the music~~
    that harrowing sound   gathering
                    creeping
              towards

    a body
    yet to learn
    to dance
        only how to hide
    cadence   crawling   closer

a cloak   of full-grown
flesh   smothers a boy
left shaken   by his imagination

hands over ears
    eyes shut tight

        & only then
            the thunder comes

Azanian Abecedarian (with Eyes)

*'We know too well that our freedom is incomplete without
the freedom of the Palestinians.' – Nelson Mandela*

Azania, how do you so easily turn your face away?
blinded / silence piercing your ears / collective roof of mouths
caved in / really? nothing more to say? / even through a sea of red-
dot recordings / remnants remind us / of our own haunting:
eyes have seen this all before / / amid the struggle for our
freedom / does sunlight carry radiance across the troubled skies of
Gaza? / beyond the mushroom clouds / beyond plague of power blocking
humanity / even before the siege / there existed a threat of being
impaled by the sharp edges of tyranny / & when they use the word
justice / how does it taste? / is it as sweet as a forehead
kissed / amid the bitterness of war / while the children fear
living perpetually as statues / and how come their safe zones seem to
move when the people move? / is this how the magnets of the
Nakba keep pulling? / / Azania, do your eyes see beyond the dark depths
of a hole? / can you still hear echoes of Mandela as he spoke / of
Palestinian freedom as being adjacent to our own? / / and in the
quest for fulfilment / how do we carry on without thinking of a
river / whose waters merge with tears / if only to will it closer to the
sea / / Azania, how do you keep your head down? / you so easily
turn your face away / have you forgotten the meaning of
ubuntu? / are you so undone at the hands of a strange love / a
violent love for the bomb / / where would we be if the
world also chose to look away? / to go contrary to our
xenophobia / don't our differences make us all the same / / pain of all the
years / of overcast clouds covering / grey wound of heaven
zulu vuleka / wash away the hurt / wash away this pain

Baw Baw (One for the Black Sheep)

black sheep so willing
to shear your own dark wool
to convince the eyes gazing upon you
that you too are worthy of love

behold a thread unravelling
a glass ceiling untouched
hands burrowing beneath
a heavy burden of proof

all you have ever known
was a golden child
whose body blocked your sun,
your thick black wool
eclipsed at every turn

black sheep for so long
you've lived under the sun
to the point that you've made peace
with embodying a shadow

if young lambs lose their way
only the tender bleating of the ewe
will lead them home

a voice resonates with the ram in agony
so fluent in the language of pain
how different it all could have been
if only for the nurturing

In The Presence of Ocean Water

in the presence of ocean water
my occipital bone held down
hands placed gently on the skull

a widening palm cupped the skull
a man of the cloth attempts to heal me
a man of the cloth attempts to kill me

the end, a promise for eternal life
the other, a threat made towards my life
while plunged into the depth of the ocean

clear bottled rituals, collected ocean
the deja-vu of having been here before
the deja-vu of having done this before

could death teach the boy to swim
through a lifetime of struggling to swim
through his mind, he is drowning

out of his mouth, he is drowning

Swimming versus Drowning

nobody tells you how
the art of drowning
each harsh stroke
leads you deeper into
the sudden realisation
of all the loss at sea
the bottom of the ocean
could well be the place
for the body's eternal sleep

it all begins from a body
pulling downwards
on calm waters
the meditative parts
of an ocean
filled with
boundless possibilities
to discover the will to float
or the minds transcendence

underwater
your hands moving
the forced ripples
of soul
& all its depth
the undiscovered self
the water
a lesson on destiny
towards the art of swimming

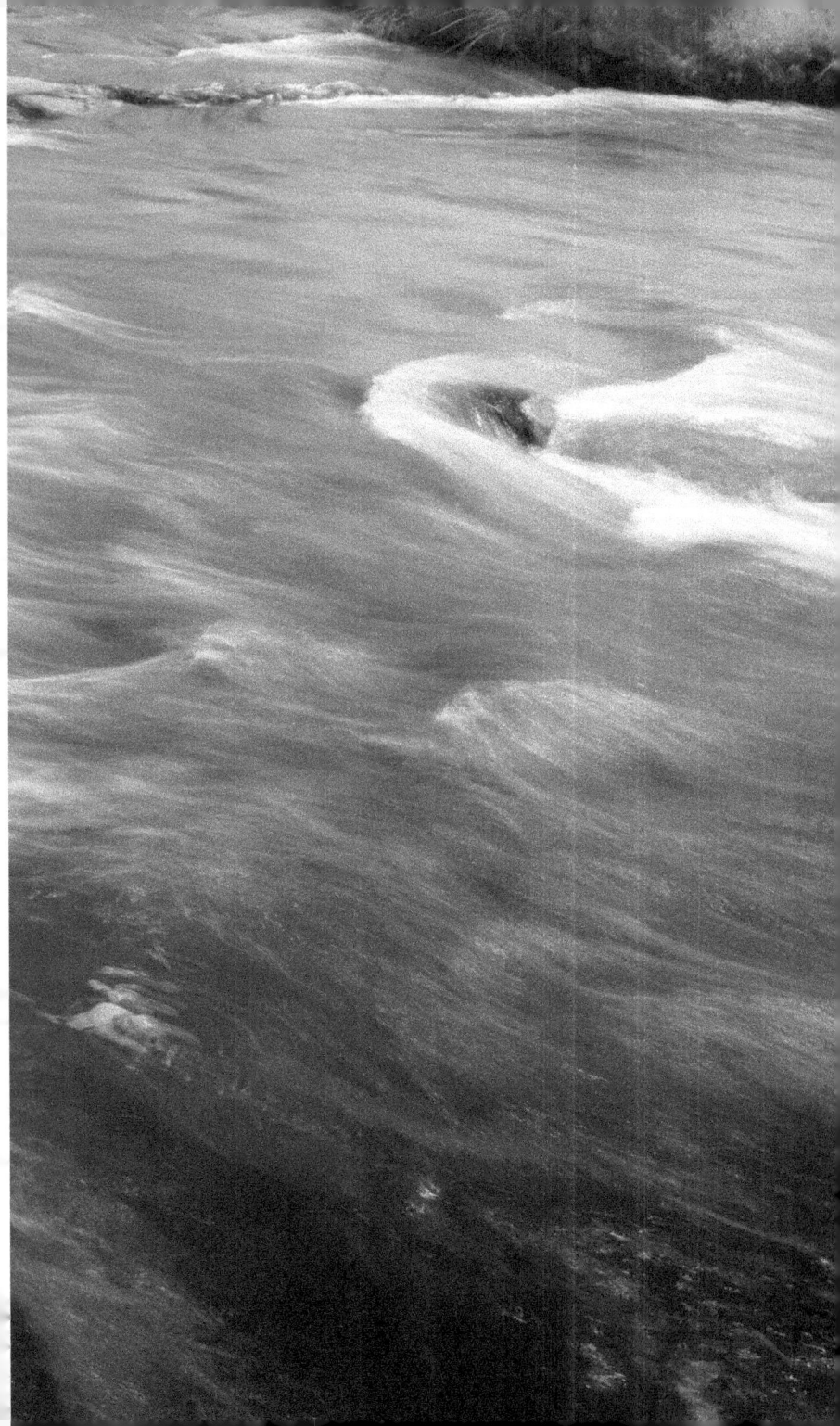

ULWANDLE LWASENDIYA

ngalo lelo langa sahlukana ngasolwandle / imifula yaKwaZulu
isihlangene isiyongena emlonyeni wolwandle / wona lo ohambayo
uze uyozilahla kwelaseNdiya / lapho amanzi efika efudumele
okwegazi / lona leli elizogijima emzimbeni sekuliwa / izikhalazo
zezinhlungu zahamba / zadlula ngaphezu kwamanzi / kwathula
ngisho neculo legagasi / sezwa ngamehlo ethu abheke ngasolwandle
ezibuza ethi, kaze ukuthula kuzobuya nini? / sesibuyela / kuyo
lendaba yokuhlukana / yona eyaqala ngokuphikisana kwezinhlanga
abansundu namaNdiya ngamakhanda bangqubuzana / abanye
bawela emanzini / bona labo ulwandle waqanjwa ngabo / thina
zingane zohlanga / sawela ngomhlane kumhlaba / sahlukana kanjalo.

Lunga

zaqala ziwutshani, zaphenduka ameva
zagwaza amafu, zawisa kwemvula
zasho zathi: nalokhu bekumele kwenezeke
zaphela izinhlungu, sabona sekulunga

You Are the Elders Now

our family is changing who will hold what our ancestors once held firm? the stories they told about the sanctity of lines our lineage who is left now to carry this for them?

consider this: we give thought to superstitions and then they come alive the sun as kin to fire birth begins first with bones tender to hard to tender once again & is it the fear of all this that leads us to move away?

again consider: ngaphansi kwethu, a black heaven bare soles connecting us like roots hard to break the tar rigid roads underfoot yet even through all this their whispers still come to us saying *you are the elders now.*

Aubade to the Natural Light & The Revelation of Love

before our pending illumination
amid bruised ceiling of earth / as the night sky concealed our love
when only the songs of the cicada survived

& all that held our eyelids open
our fear to close them / on the chance fate might befall us too soon
a periphery unbearable / our dream to live sincere

interlude calming song of morning
& all we really had was patience

no longer could night deny our sky of its loosening
sharp piercing entry of the joy
bleeding golden through the clouds

Mamkhulu

amid the disrepair / before functioning hands *returned*
the wisdom of clocks / a lesson *returned*

in exchange / a redeeming of your breath
my circadian rhythm resumed / your voice *returned*

& as it once was / the familiar speaking life into me
ancestor elevating / eyes reopened / a sunshine *returned*

I cry not knowing how much longer we have together
vow to hold you tight / past a moon *returned*

cold child covered by the body
the mother / the sacrifice / when warmth *returned*

voodoo child foreshadowing / the slight return
one last thing / before your silence *returned*

mamkhulu / from my mouth / I fear my word love
lives with only you / sala nomshana before his fate *returned*

before uSihle is crushed under your silence
your living breath back to the past / a lesson *returned*

Ode to the Wind Blowing Gently Over Our Wounds

strokes / blows of wind
withhold stillness
legs ache for pause
knots of air untied

an invisible jolt
a delicate push
closer to, rather than
away from

lips blow down
chamomile heat
moves towards
warm / soul nourishing

eyes closed & gathering
hope with gale force
formations of tenderness
bless blues ballads
soaking our redness
so we could once again
reaffirm our love

bless the wind
blowing gently over
our wounds, & finally bless
the mouth that chose
to name this wind
time

The Brother Moves On

do you remember?

        when we were younger
        ugogo gathering pawpaw from her garden
        sitting patiently   waiting
        for us to finish   indulging   in the fruit
        knowing full well
                that her grandsons
        would only want more
        and with the very last one
            she plunged
            the knife deep inside
            cutting it in two

the way she sat close by
            and watched us
            tasting rich textures
            of a tropical delicacy,
            & once we had our fill
                she imparted wisdom
                    the necessity to share
        with one another

reminding us
        that when we entered this world
            we entered it together as twins
        amawele
            and that twins
                was how God had intended it to be

                that you and I
                    were born this way
                            for a reason
lest we forget
            her lesson in the garden
            much later in life I would learn
            that our late grandmother decided on our names
            in much the same way,
            after   you entered   this world   first
            it was ugogo who decided
            that my name
                        would be on the end of yours
a reminder
            that even when we separate
                        we will remain together always

    brother,
        I know
        how life
        can often
        feel like
        years
        of accumulating
        soil,
        burying us alive,

    and on that day in the garden

I felt the words
    of our grandmother,
            as her bare hands
            in brown soil
            delicately
            placed a seed
            deep
            within us

            in a place
            where hope
      can live

    her hope
          that someday
    for us
    a soaring tree
    with leaves   protruding
    from tender parts
    of the chest

    a bond   as strong
    as the oak tree
          towering over
          providing shade
          from a harsh sun
    and so, brother
          with this in mind
    I must ask you   once more

do you remember?

Ngizizwa Ngingenwa Uvalo

seliguqubele, amacala abo avusa abadala bethu abalele,
ekushoneni kwelanga, ngizizwa ngingenwa uvalo
ave besaba, bathi sifuna ukuphindisela,
kaze yiso yini, isimnyama sabo sesiyangena?

NOTES

I would like to acknowledge the sources and partial sources of the following poems:

- "Nganekwane" refers to a viral video featuring Sandile Mtshali, shown in a reflector vest, attempting to tell a folktale to a group of uninterested men; the italicised words in the poem are a direct quotation from the video. The poem also makes reference to the 2000 film *Crouching Tiger, Hidden Dragon*, directed by Ang Lee.
- "Langa" is based on an interview with Ousmane Sembène in a 1983 documentary titled *Caméra D'Afrique*, directed by Férid Boughedir.
- The title of "Darkie Fiction" refers to the eponymous Johannesburg-based musicians.
- "The Infinite Pursuit of Booty" refers to the Bantu migrations.
- The opening portion of "Belly" refers to an interview with Thabang Moloi televised and published by eNews Channel Africa on 14 June 2022 under the title "Soweto Residents Protest". The poem also makes reference to the 1998 film *Belly*, directed by Hype Williams, as well as the music video for the 2000 song "Untitled (How Does It Feel)" by D'Angelo, directed by Paul Hunter and Dominique Trenier.
- "The Etymology of Thanda/Thando" is written after E'mon Lauren's poem "The Etymology of "CHUUCH!" which appears in the April 2018 edition of *Poetry*.
- "Mfecane" is written after Maneo Mohale's poem "Difeqane" that appears in their collection *Everything is a deathly flower* (uHlanga, 2019).

- "Kasala" is inspired by and uses elements of ritual panegyric poetry used by the Lubà people in the Democratic Republic of the Congo.
- The epigraph to "Azanian Abecedarian" quotes a speech made by Nelson Mandela at the International Day of Solidarity with Palestinian People, held in Pretoria on 4 December 1997. The full passage reads: "But we know too well that our freedom is incomplete without the freedom of the Palestinians; without the resolution of conflicts in East Timor, the Sudan and other parts of the world." The poem also refers to the 1964 film *Dr. Strangelove or: How I Learned to Stop Worrying and Love the Bomb*, directed by Stanley Kubrick.
- "Swimming versus Drowning" is a contrapuntal poem.
- The title of "The Brother Moves On" is a reference to the eponymous Johannesburg-based performance art ensemble.

SOUTH AFRICAN POETRY SINCE 2014

— RECENT RELEASES —

a corpse is also a garden by Pieter Madibuseng Odendaal

Rootbound by Manthipe Moila

Fall Risk by Kobus Moolman

Poetry NonScenes: New performance poems beyond the Struggle, edited by Tom Penfold, Adam Levin and Deirdre Byrne

Dayspring: A Memoir by C. J. Driver, edited by J. M. Coetzee
A 2024 *NEW STATESMAN* BOOK OF THE YEAR

The Book of Unrest by Nick Mulgrew
SHORTLISTED FOR THE 2024 NIHSS AWARD FOR BEST POETRY

A Short Treatise on Mortality by Douglas Reid Skinner

Peach Country by Nondwe Mpuma
SHORTLISTED FOR THE 2023 NIHSS AWARD FOR BEST POETRY

— RECENTLY-AWARD-WINNING TITLES —

Ilifa ngu Athambile Masola
WINNER OF THE 2022 NIHSS AWARD FOR BEST POETRY

An Illuminated Darkness by Jacques Coetzee
WINNER OF THE 2022 INGRID JONKER & OLIVE SCHREINER PRIZES

All the Places by Musawenkosi Khanyile
WINNER OF THE 2021 NIHSS AWARD & 2020 SALA FOR POETRY

Everything is a deathly flower by Maneo Mohale
WINNER OF THE 2020 GLENNA LUSCHEI PRIZE FOR AFRICAN POETRY

AVAILABLE FROM GOOD BOOKSTORES IN SOUTHERN AFRICA
UHLANGAPRESS.CO.ZA

www.ingramcontent.com/pod-product-compliance
Lightning Source LLC
Chambersburg PA
CBHW070208100426
42743CB00013B/3095